RANDOM HOUSE

WORLDS
NEW YORK

Published in the United States by Random House Worlds, an imprint of Random House, a division of Penguin Random House LLC, New York.

RANDOM HOUSE is a registered trademark, and RANDOM HOUSE WORLDS and colophon are trademarks of Penguin Random House LLC.

Originally published in hardcover in the United Kingdom by Farshore, an imprint of HarperCollins Publishers Limited.

ISBN 978-0-593-59960-0
Ebook ISBN 978-0-593-59961-7

Printed in the United States on acid-free paper

randomhousebooks.com

2 4 6 8 9 7 5 3

First US Edition

Written by Thomas McBrien
Special thanks to Sherin Kwan, Alex Wiltshire, Jay Castello and Milo Bengtsson

MINECRAFT™

SUPER
BITE-SIZE
BUILDS

WITH OVER 20 EPIC MINI-PROJECTS

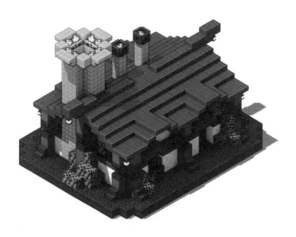

CONTENTS

INTRODUCTION

Welcome to the third installment of the Bite-Size Builds series! This book is packed with 20 new fun mini-projects for you to build in Minecraft. From igloo hideouts to mud block greenhouses and dangerous arcade games, there's a build for everyone between these pages!

No matter how good a player you are, there's always more to learn as you discover Minecraft. With exploded diagrams and detailed step-by-step instructions, this book will guide you through over 20 unique builds, providing helpful tips to ensure you can complete them all with ease. The builds vary from small to large and from simple to difficult. Check out the key on each build to find out more.

Embrace your creativity and put your own stamp on these builds. If you think your build will look better with different blocks or tweaked designs, follow your instincts and make these builds your own. Soon, you'll be showing off your incredible talent to the world around you.

GENERAL BUILD TIPS

Check out all the amazing builds in this book! There's really something for everyone, no matter your skill level. You can start with the easy builds first or dive straight into one of the more difficult builds. The choice is yours! Here are some tips to help you get started.

CREATIVE MODE

We recommend that you use Creative mode for these builds. With unlimited access to all the blocks in the game and instant block removal, Creative mode is the easiest way to build in Minecraft. If you like a challenge, each structure can be built in Survival mode, but be warned – it will take a lot more time and preparation!

BUILD PREPARATION

Before starting a build, take a moment to look at the instructions. Consider where you want to place the build and how much space you will need to complete it. You'll want to give yourself plenty of room to build!

TEMPORARY BLOCKS

Temporary building blocks are great for counting out spaces and placing floating items. Using temporary blocks will also help you with tricky block placement!

Count the dimensions using different color blocks. This row represents 13 blocks: 5 green + 5 yellow + 3 green.

Use temporary blocks to help place floating blocks.

HOTBARS

Most builds use lots of different materials. You can prepare your blocks in the hotbar before starting for quick access, and if you don't have enough space, you can save up to nine hotbars in the inventory window.

BLOCK PLACEMENT

Placing a block beside an interactive one, such as an enchanting table, can be tricky. By clicking to place a block, you'll interact with the interactive one instead. Thankfully, there is a trick to avoid this! Crouch first and then click to place your block. Simple!

WARDROBE PORTAL

There is more to this wardrobe than meets the eye. Open its huge doors, shuffle your way past the hanging banners ... and find yourself transported to the Nether! This wardrobe adds magic and mystery to a Nether portal, hiding it away in plain sight.

DIFFICULTY:
★☆☆☆☆
🕐 15 mins

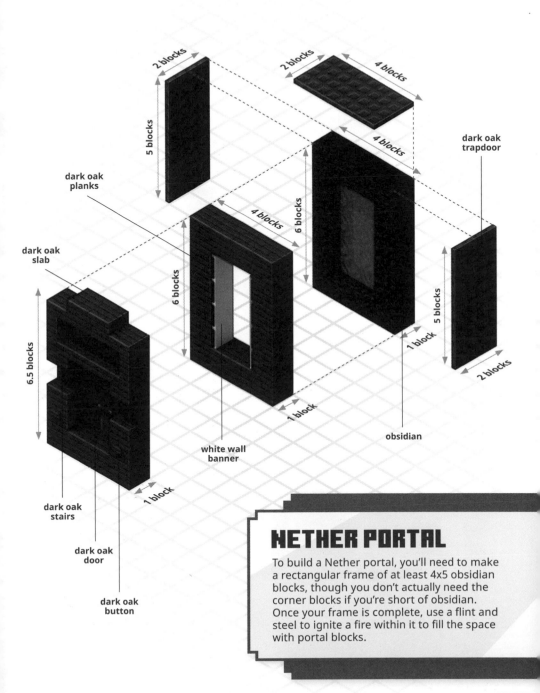

2 blocks

5 blocks

2 blocks

4 blocks

dark oak
trapdoor

dark oak
planks

4 blocks

4 blocks

6 blocks

dark oak
slab

6 blocks

6 blocks

5 blocks

6.5 blocks

1 block

1 block

white wall
banner

1 block

obsidian

dark oak
stairs

dark oak
door

1 block

dark oak
button

NETHER PORTAL

To build a Nether portal, you'll need to make
a rectangular frame of at least 4x5 obsidian
blocks, though you don't actually need the
corner blocks if you're short of obsidian.
Once your frame is complete, use a flint and
steel to ignite a fire within it to fill the space
with portal blocks.

PIG HOT-AIR BALLOON

Oink oink! As if hot-air balloons weren't already the most beautiful way to fly, here we've created the cutest way to take to the skies with this fun pig hot-air balloon! Sure, this build doesn't actually fly anywhere, but just think how amazing it will look tethered next to your base!

DIFFICULTY:
★★☆☆☆
🕐 15 mins

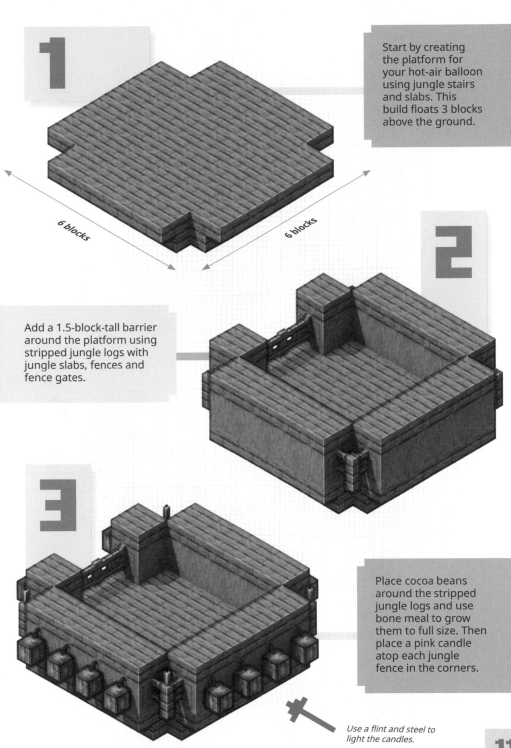

1

Start by creating the platform for your hot-air balloon using jungle stairs and slabs. This build floats 3 blocks above the ground.

6 blocks

6 blocks

2

Add a 1.5-block-tall barrier around the platform using stripped jungle logs with jungle slabs, fences and fence gates.

3

Place cocoa beans around the stripped jungle logs and use bone meal to grow them to full size. Then place a pink candle atop each jungle fence in the corners.

Use a flint and steel to light the candles.

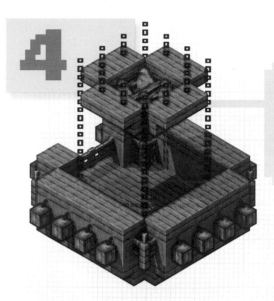

4

Next, start building the burner for the hot-air balloon. Place chains in 5-block-tall vertical links in each corner of the basket. Then create the burner using jungle stairs, jungle slabs and campfires, and more chains on top to connect to the balloon.

5

Now move on to the balloon itself. Create an 8x8 pink concrete platform with a 2x2 gap in the middle as shown.

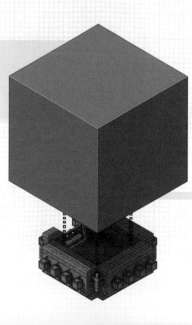

6

Add three walls and a roof to the 8x8 pink concrete platform until you have a large, hollow cube.

7

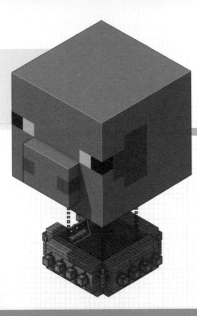

Finally, use white wool, black wool and pink terracotta to give your hot-air balloon its distinctive details. This one looks like a pig!

BUZZ BUZZ

You can create lots of different designs for your hot-air balloon, styled on each of the mob heads. Why not try to create your own? Follow these designs for your own bee and Enderman hot-air balloons.

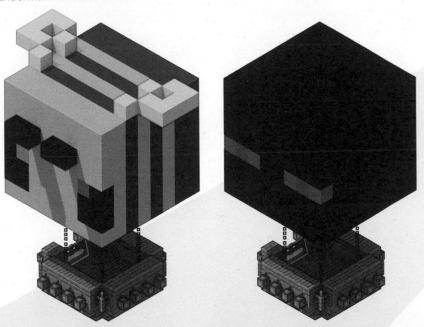

BIG RED BARN

So you've gone and created yourself fields upon fields of wheat, stretching as far as a spyglass can see. It sounds dreamy! But what are you to do with all that wheat? There's far too much for bread alone. This barn and silo could be the perfect answer to your granary needs.

DIFFICULTY:
★★★☆☆
🕐 35 mins

14

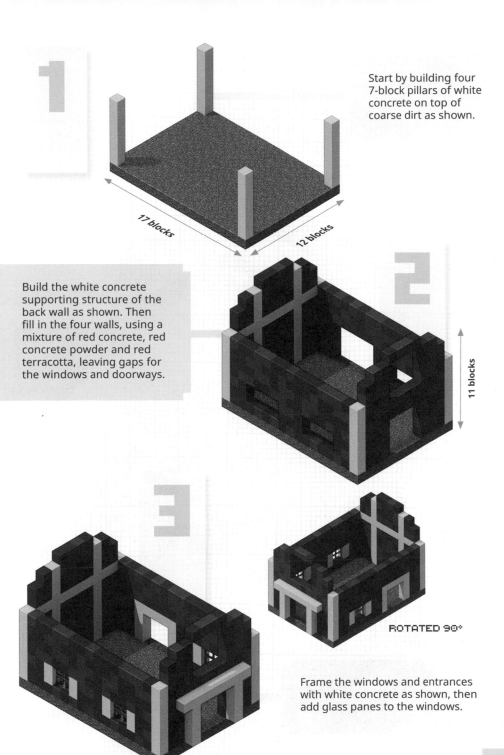

1 Start by building four 7-block pillars of white concrete on top of coarse dirt as shown.

17 blocks

12 blocks

Build the white concrete supporting structure of the back wall as shown. Then fill in the four walls, using a mixture of red concrete, red concrete powder and red terracotta, leaving gaps for the windows and doorways.

2

11 blocks

3

ROTATED 90°

Frame the windows and entrances with white concrete as shown, then add glass panes to the windows.

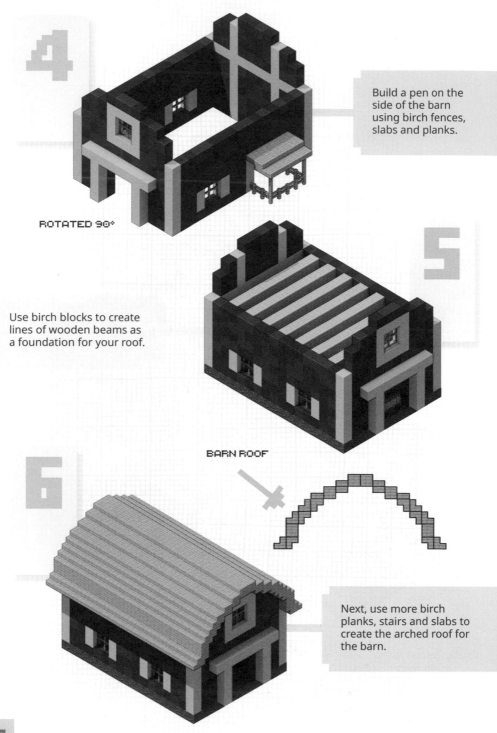

4

ROTATED 90°

Build a pen on the side of the barn using birch fences, slabs and planks.

5

Use birch blocks to create lines of wooden beams as a foundation for your roof.

BARN ROOF

6

Next, use more birch planks, stairs and slabs to create the arched roof for the barn.

GODA BASE

lots of space but tired of the same old structures? This pagoda
ming with character. It is four stories tall with each floor following
ar style for a simple yet classy finish. Did you know pagodas are
ed by their eaves and tiered floors?

Then, with more red concrete, red concrete powder and red terracotta, start building a chimney for ventilating the barn. Complete the chimney using birch stairs, planks and fences.

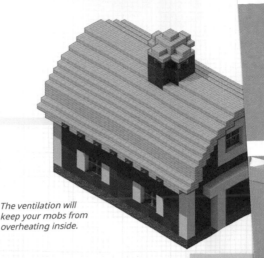

The ventilation will keep your mobs from overheating inside.

P[

Need
is te
a sim
defir

BONUS SI[

Why not add this silo
Silos are used on farr
feed for the animals.
yours with chests for

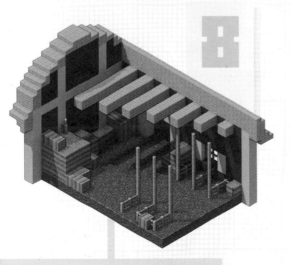

Finally, complete the interior of the barn using birch fences and hay bales to create stalls. Remember to light up the interior with torches.

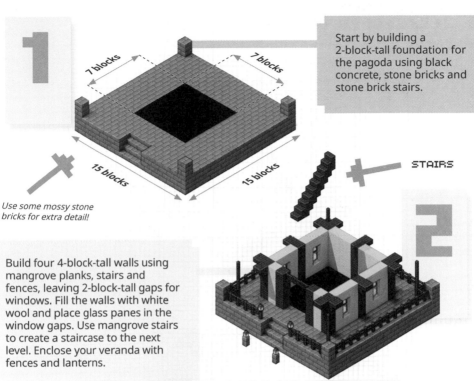

1

7 blocks — 7 blocks

15 blocks — 15 blocks

Start by building a 2-block-tall foundation for the pagoda using black concrete, stone bricks and stone brick stairs.

Use some mossy stone bricks for extra detail!

STAIRS

2

Build four 4-block-tall walls using mangrove planks, stairs and fences, leaving 2-block-tall gaps for windows. Fill the walls with white wool and place glass panes in the window gaps. Use mangrove stairs to create a staircase to the next level. Enclose your veranda with fences and lanterns.

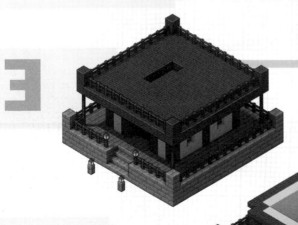

3

Next, build the second floor of the pagoda structure using mangrove planks and fences. Make sure you connect the floor to the fences in the foundation from step 2.

4

Add a second 4-walled room using mangrove planks, stairs and slabs. Create a lip around the top for the copper eaves to go on.

Then add another floor above step 4 with cut copper slabs and stairs for eaves, and more mangrove planks. Use ladders to connect the levels together.

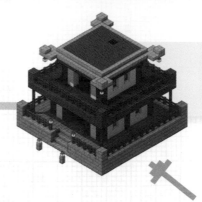

5

You could use honeycomb to wax the copper instead, so it doesn't age!

6

Add a third 4-walled room with eaves, directly above the last, using the same blocks as steps 4 and 5.

This floor reintroduces windows to the build. This is a simple but effective method for adding details to big structures.

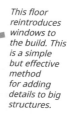

Add a fourth room with eaves directly above step 6, again using the same blocks. Remember to link all the floors with ladders inside.

7

8

Build the fifth and final 4-block-tall room of the pagoda on your remaining footprint with more of the same blocks.

9

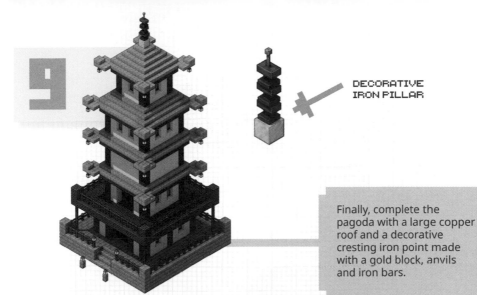

DECORATIVE
IRON PILLAR

Finally, complete the pagoda with a large copper roof and a decorative cresting iron point made with a gold block, anvils and iron bars.

INTERIOR

With five tiered rooms to the pagoda, there is tons of space for storing all your treasures. As you're going to spend so much time sorting through your chests, you may as well be comfortable while doing so! Decorate the bottom two floors with something like this.

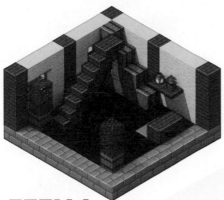

ROOM 1

The ground floor should have all the items you need in a rush, so barrels are the perfect solution. Add a simple desk using stair blocks and decorate with some plants to make the space homey.

ROOM 2

The second floor is where you'll plan your next adventure – standing safely above any zombies who decide to follow you inside! Another desk and a few more barrels and you're all set!

IGLOO HIDEOUT

Brrrr ... it can get pretty cold in these snowy biomes, even with a pair of warm leather boots to keep your feet dry. There may not be a lot of resources to build with here, but there is plenty of snow. Build this igloo and fill it with lots of wool to make it feel warm and cozy.

DIFFICULTY:
★★★☆☆
🕐 35 mins

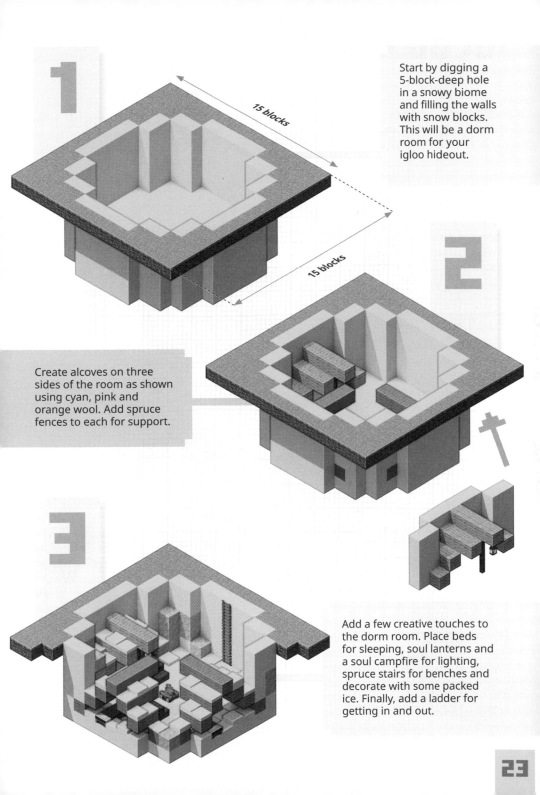

1

15 blocks

15 blocks

Start by digging a 5-block-deep hole in a snowy biome and filling the walls with snow blocks. This will be a dorm room for your igloo hideout.

2

Create alcoves on three sides of the room as shown using cyan, pink and orange wool. Add spruce fences to each for support.

3

Add a few creative touches to the dorm room. Place beds for sleeping, soul lanterns and a soul campfire for lighting, spruce stairs for benches and decorate with some packed ice. Finally, add a ladder for getting in and out.

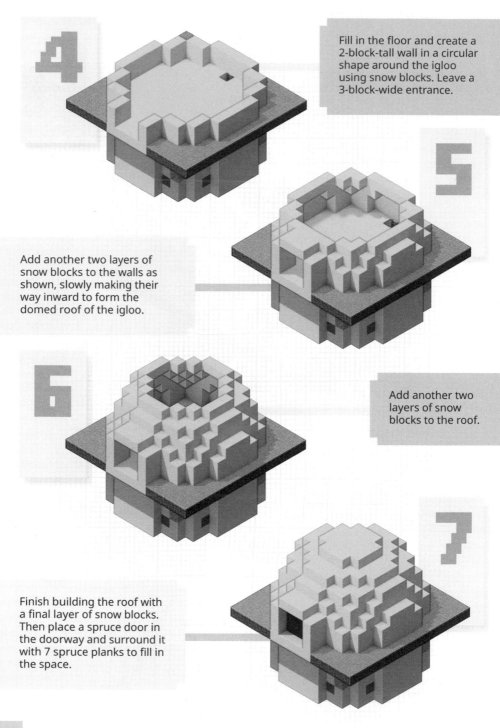

4

Fill in the floor and create a 2-block-tall wall in a circular shape around the igloo using snow blocks. Leave a 3-block-wide entrance.

5

Add another two layers of snow blocks to the walls as shown, slowly making their way inward to form the domed roof of the igloo.

6

Add another two layers of snow blocks to the roof.

7

Finish building the roof with a final layer of snow blocks. Then place a spruce door in the doorway and surround it with 7 spruce planks to fill in the space.

INTERIOR

Just because the snowy biome is chilly and white outside doesn't mean this has to be reflected on the inside of your igloo. Add these finishing touches to make your build warm, colorful and inviting.

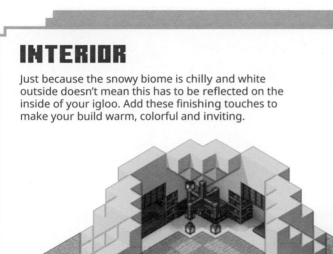

Light up the room with a soul lantern chandelier. The blue glow will illuminate your snowy igloo with an eerie blue light.

Build reading nooks using spruce planks, bookshelves and barrels. The barrels are the perfect place to store your adventuring journals when you're out exploring.

A nice, thick carpet will keep your toes warm. Why not try this design using the same pink, orange and cyan colors from the dorm below?

ALLAY STATUE

These wonderful little mobs love nothing more than to fly around helping you. Give one an item and they'll do everything they can to bring you more of them. Like allays, this statue glows in the dark, making it a perfect depiction of this cute companion.

DIFFICULTY:
★☆☆☆☆
🕐 10 mins

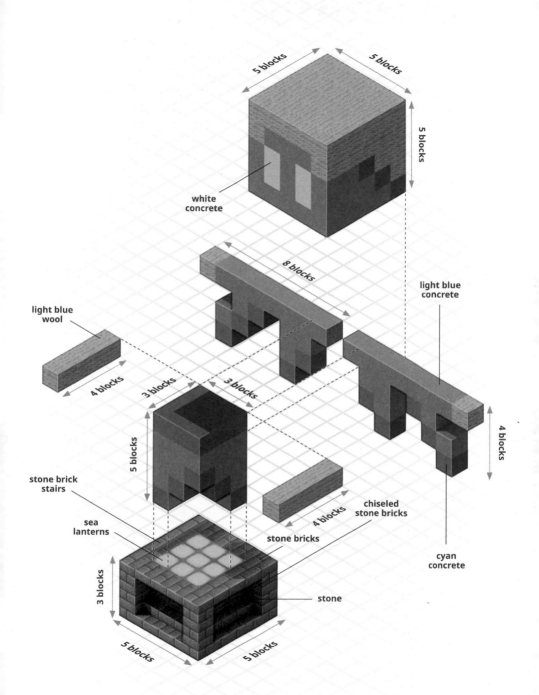

5 blocks
5 blocks
5 blocks

white
concrete

8 blocks

light blue
concrete

light blue
wool

4 blocks

3 blocks

3 blocks

4 blocks

5 blocks

stone brick
stairs

chiseled
stone bricks

4 blocks

sea
lanterns

stone bricks

cyan
concrete

3 blocks

stone

5 blocks

5 blocks

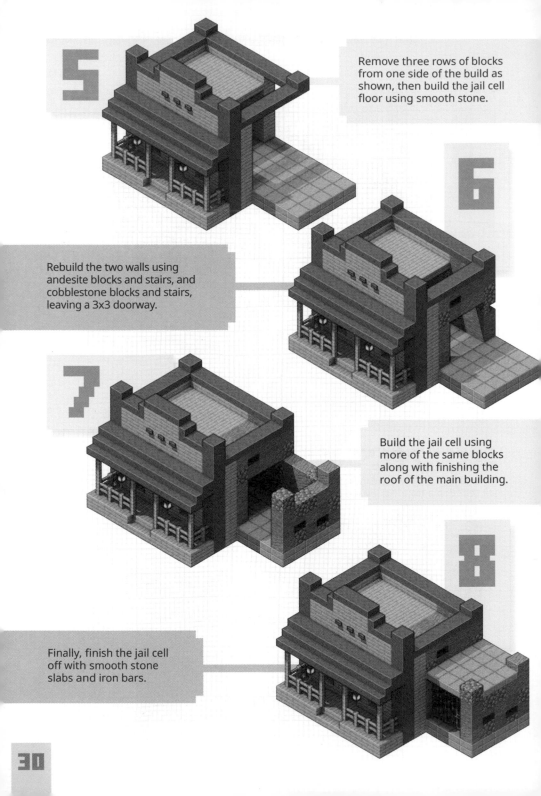

5

Remove three rows of blocks from one side of the build as shown, then build the jail cell floor using smooth stone.

6

Rebuild the two walls using andesite blocks and stairs, and cobblestone blocks and stairs, leaving a 3x3 doorway.

7

Build the jail cell using more of the same blocks along with finishing the roof of the main building.

8

Finally, finish the jail cell off with smooth stone slabs and iron bars.

INTERIOR

Don't forget to finish the interiors! For this jailhouse to be in functioning order, there are a few more necessities.

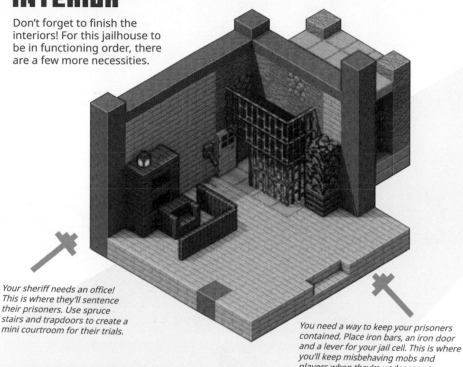

Your sheriff needs an office! This is where they'll sentence their prisoners. Use spruce stairs and trapdoors to create a mini courtroom for their trials.

You need a way to keep your prisoners contained. Place iron bars, an iron door and a lever for your jail cell. This is where you'll keep misbehaving mobs and players when they're under arrest.

SECRET PASSAGE

Why not get creative and imagine a pesky prisoner has dug an escape tunnel from your jail cell? Pop a trapdoor over it, though, so your new prisoners don't find it!

Fill your escape tunnel with water, so no one will think anything of it from the outside!

SECRET ISLAND BASE

There are well over 2,000 unique tropical fish variants in Minecraft. That's a whole lot of fish! See how many you can spot from the comfort of your very own secret viewing room, hidden beneath a remote island way out in the ocean. Don't forget to pack a snack!

DIFFICULTY:
★★★★★
🕐 30 mins

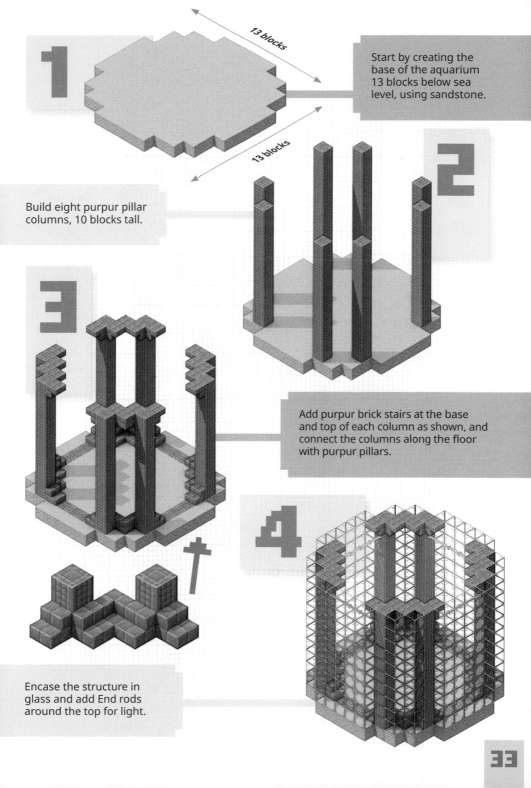

1 Start by creating the base of the aquarium 13 blocks below sea level, using sandstone.

13 blocks

13 blocks

Build eight purpur pillar columns, 10 blocks tall.

2

3

Add purpur brick stairs at the base and top of each column as shown, and connect the columns along the floor with purpur pillars.

4

Encase the structure in glass and add End rods around the top for light.

Fill the aquarium with sand then delete the blocks to remove the water. Complete the aquarium structure with another layer of sandstone, leaving two gaps for the water elevators a block apart in the center.

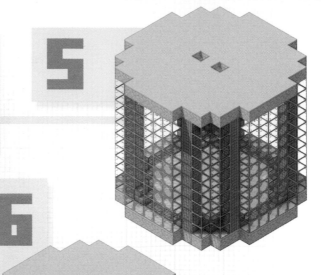

5

6

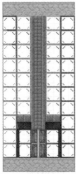 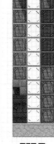

FRONT   SIDE

Inside the aquarium, build the purpur-and-glass elevator shafts. Place a soul sand block beneath one shaft and a magma block below the other. Place 2 doors and 2 End rods at the base.

7

Place a layer of sand and two layers of grass above the aquarium leaving gaps above the elevator shafts.

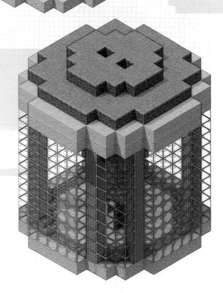

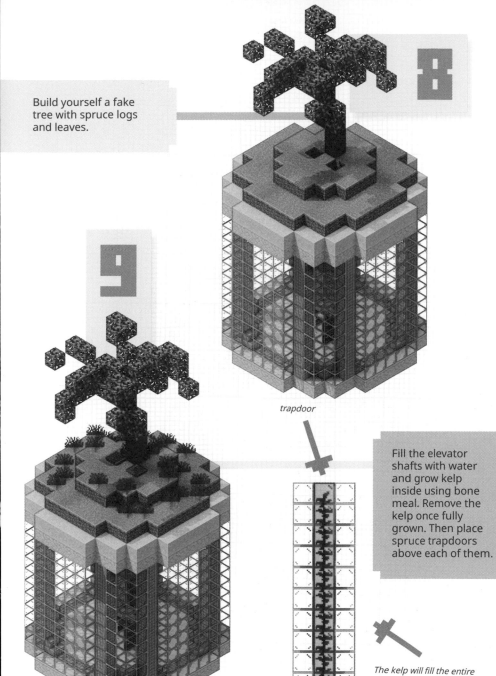

Build yourself a fake tree with spruce logs and leaves.

8

9

trapdoor

Fill the elevator shafts with water and grow kelp inside using bone meal. Remove the kelp once fully grown. Then place spruce trapdoors above each of them.

The kelp will fill the entire elevator shaft with water sources and activate the bubble columns.

soul sand

ELEVATOR SHAFTS

GREENHOUSE

With heaps of fruit, vegetables and plants to discover in Minecraft, what better way to grow your favorites than from the comfort of a greenhouse? This mud brick build will have you feeling at one with nature long before you plant your first seed.

DIFFICULTY:
★★★☆☆

🕐 35 mins

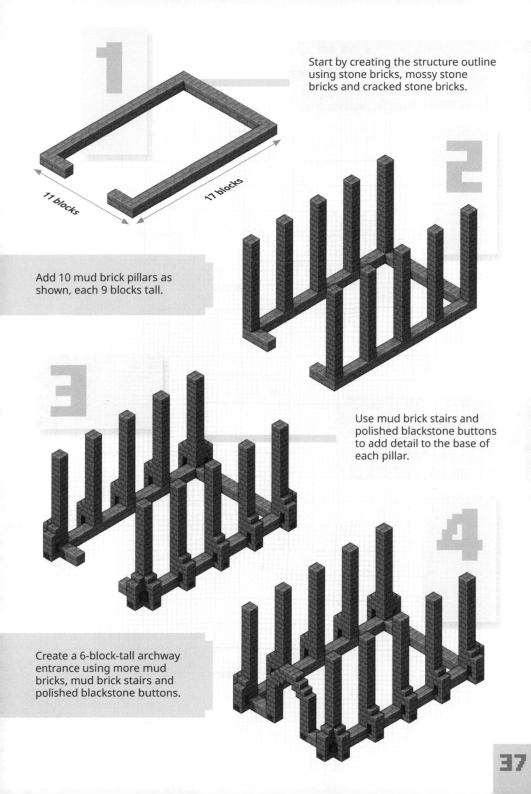

1 Start by creating the structure outline using stone bricks, mossy stone bricks and cracked stone bricks.

11 blocks

17 blocks

2 Add 10 mud brick pillars as shown, each 9 blocks tall.

3 Use mud brick stairs and polished blackstone buttons to add detail to the base of each pillar.

4 Create a 6-block-tall archway entrance using more mud bricks, mud brick stairs and polished blackstone buttons.

5

Start building the pointed roof with mud brick stairs and slabs.

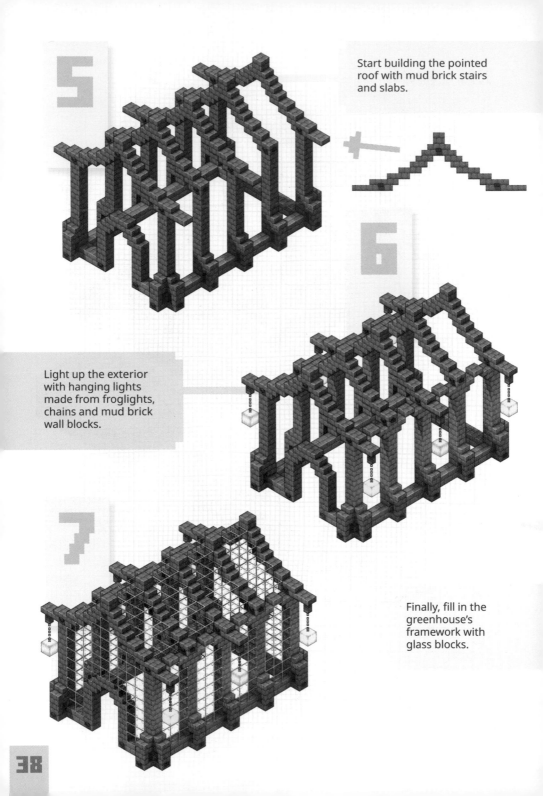

Light up the exterior with hanging lights made from froglights, chains and mud brick wall blocks.

6

7

Finally, fill in the greenhouse's framework with glass blocks.

INTERIOR

This greenhouse is almost ready to grow plants in! All it needs now is a bit of sprucing up inside.

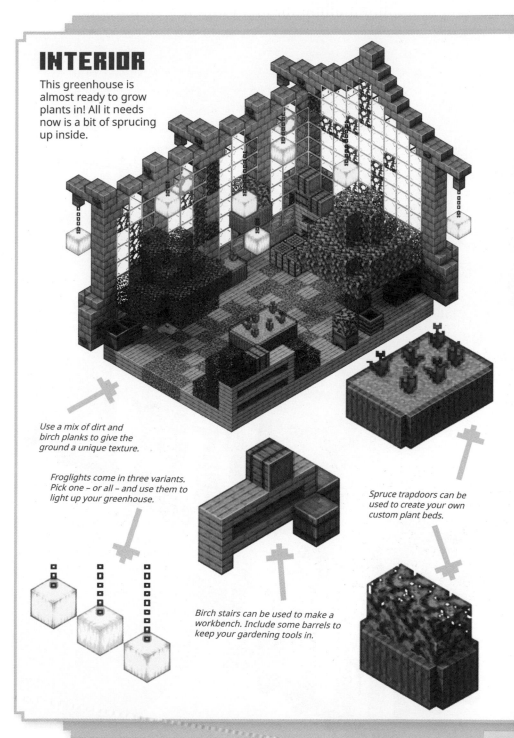

Use a mix of dirt and birch planks to give the ground a unique texture.

Froglights come in three variants. Pick one – or all – and use them to light up your greenhouse.

Spruce trapdoors can be used to create your own custom plant beds.

Birch stairs can be used to make a workbench. Include some barrels to keep your gardening tools in.

STEAMBOAT

All aboard! Get your tickets stamped and find your seats; this luxury river steamboat will be setting off downstream in no time. Invite guests for fine dining on the river or put on a music show to the sound of lapping water. This triple-deck steamer can be used for whatever floats your boat!

DIFFICULTY:
★★★☆☆
🕐 35 mins

1

The hull of the ship sits 1 block below water level.

22 blocks

9 blocks

Start by building the steamboat's base hull using gray concrete and glass blocks as shown.

2

Fill the hull with all the storage you need, using a mix of barrels and chests. At the back of the riverboat, use blast furnaces, smokers and grindstones to create the "engine." Don't forget a ladder to the upper deck!

3

Build the first deck out of smooth quartz, gray concrete and birch slabs.

4

Add a 2-block-tall central cabin in the middle of the boat using smooth quartz, gray concrete and sets of 4 smooth quartz stairs to frame the windows. Place a birch fence gate in the entrance.

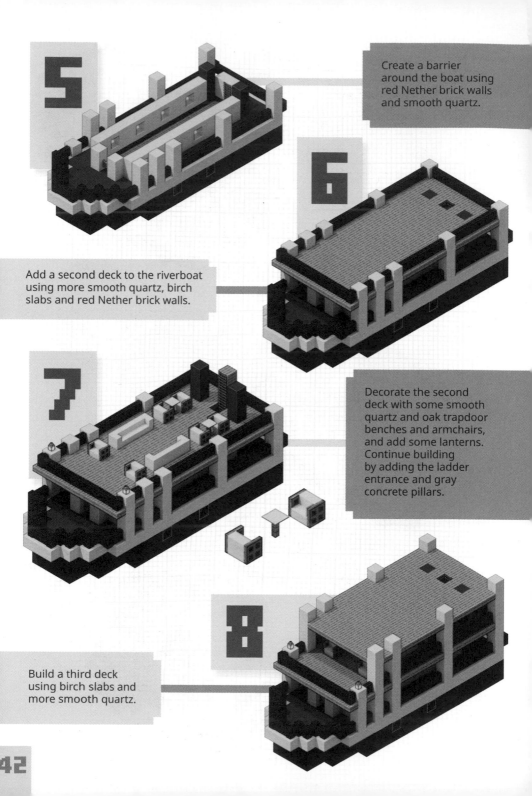

5 Create a barrier around the boat using red Nether brick walls and smooth quartz.

6 Add a second deck to the riverboat using more smooth quartz, birch slabs and red Nether brick walls.

7 Decorate the second deck with some smooth quartz and oak trapdoor benches and armchairs, and add some lanterns. Continue building by adding the ladder entrance and gray concrete pillars.

8 Build a third deck using birch slabs and more smooth quartz.

9

Decorate the third deck with more armchairs and lanterns. Use a grindstone to create the steering wheel. Then extend the ladder and gray concrete pillars again.

10

Finally, build a 7x7 birch slab roof and chimneys as shown.

The chimneys are made of campfires surrounded by oak trapdoors.

11

Use a pattern of red Nether brick blocks and stairs with a smooth quartz block in the center to create your steamboat's signature wheels.

PARKOUR PACHINKO GAME

We've taken this popular Japanese arcade game and turned it on its head. Instead of a ball tumbling down the machine, you are the ball bouncing your way up it. Hop, skip and jump your way up to victory. Careful, though! One wrong step or jump will see you plummeting into the lava below!

DIFFICULTY:
★★★★★
🕑 30 mins

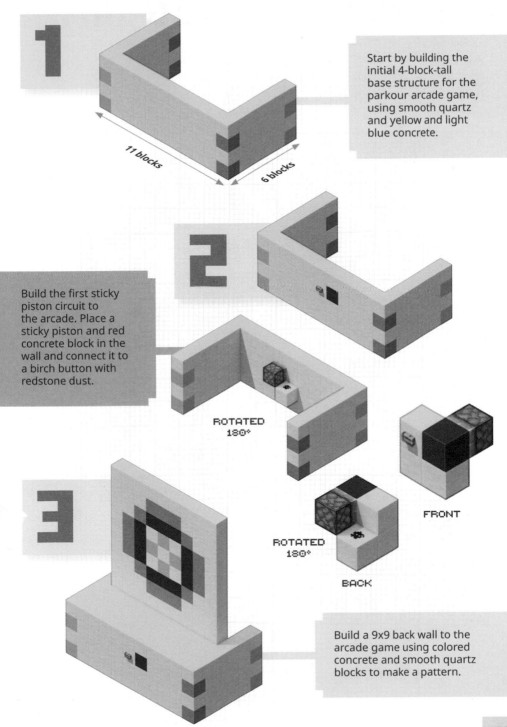

1

11 blocks

6 blocks

Start by building the initial 4-block-tall base structure for the parkour arcade game, using smooth quartz and yellow and light blue concrete.

2

Build the first sticky piston circuit to the arcade. Place a sticky piston and red concrete block in the wall and connect it to a birch button with redstone dust.

ROTATED 180°

FRONT

ROTATED 180°

BACK

3

Build a 9x9 back wall to the arcade game using colored concrete and smooth quartz blocks to make a pattern.

4

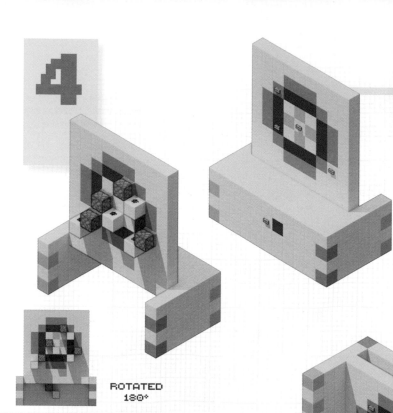

Add another 4 sticky piston circuits along the wall like in step 2.

ROTATED 180°

5

Build a wall that wraps around three sides of the top section of the build, leaving a gap for a doorway as shown.

6

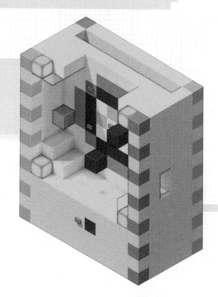

Next, add the final touches to the parkour route. Place more red and blue concrete as shown, then add smooth quartz as steps in each corner. Add lighting with sea lanterns.

Using deepslate brick stairs, slabs and walls, build a ring around the front of the arcade game to frame it. Now add the perilous lava at the bottom!

Add one more layer of concrete, smooth quartz and deepslate brick walls on top of the build. Leave a hole and place a ladder leading into and out of the game.

Lastly, place an iron door and button in the side wall, then build a staircase leading up to it. Leave a break in the staircase for players to jump using the first sticky piston circuit.

HORSE RACECOURSE

Do you have what it takes to become the best horse rider in Minecraft? Start practicing with your very own racecourse! This guide is split into three stages, so you can design your racecourse in whatever formation you prefer. Begin with the starting line and see what you create!

DIFFICULTY:
★★★★☆
🕐 1hour +

SECTION 1
STARTING LINE

Every race track needs a place to begin. This redstone starting line will ensure no one gets a head start.

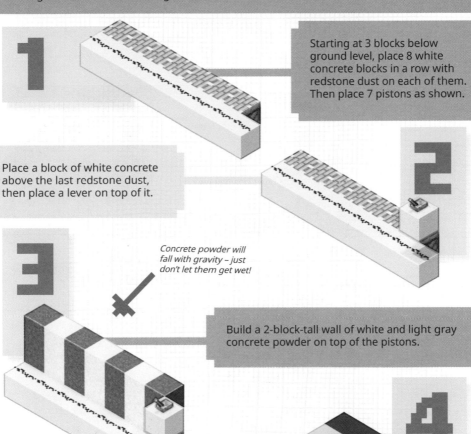

1 Starting at 3 blocks below ground level, place 8 white concrete blocks in a row with redstone dust on each of them. Then place 7 pistons as shown.

Place a block of white concrete above the last redstone dust, then place a lever on top of it.

2

3

Concrete powder will fall with gravity – just don't let them get wet!

Build a 2-block-tall wall of white and light gray concrete powder on top of the pistons.

4

Build the rest of your starting line around the redstone mechanism using gray and white concrete blocks.

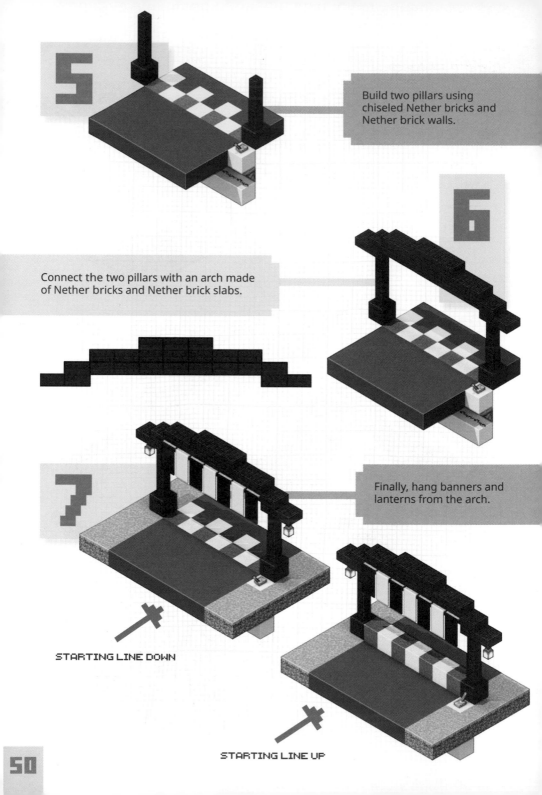

5

Build two pillars using chiseled Nether bricks and Nether brick walls.

6

Connect the two pillars with an arch made of Nether bricks and Nether brick slabs.

7

Finally, hang banners and lanterns from the arch.

STARTING LINE DOWN

STARTING LINE UP

SECTION 2
RACECOURSE

Design your own racecourse using these guides. Create as many twists and turns as you like; just remember to finish back at the starting line.

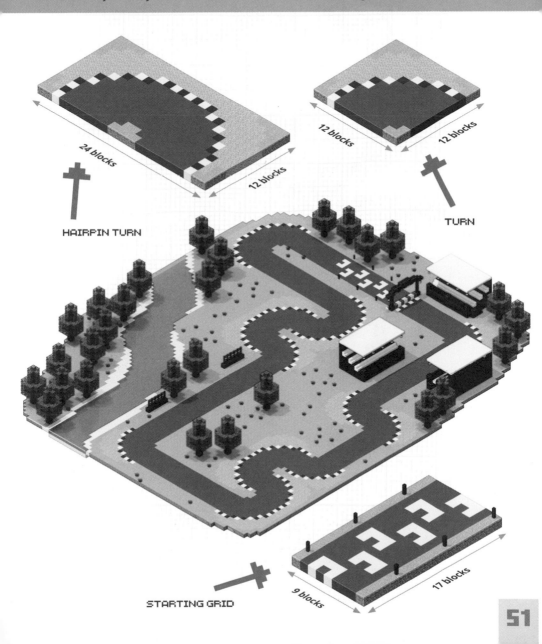

24 blocks

12 blocks

HAIRPIN TURN

12 blocks

12 blocks

TURN

9 blocks

17 blocks

STARTING GRID

Use these instructions to build grandstands around your racecourse.
Place them near the finish line, so spectators can witness the race's end.

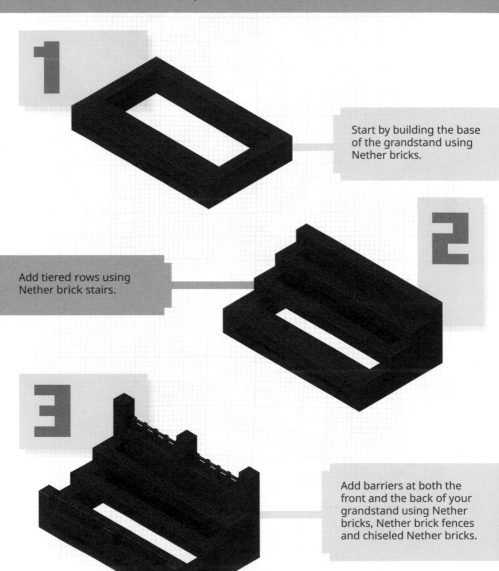

1

Start by building the base of the grandstand using Nether bricks.

2

Add tiered rows using Nether brick stairs.

3

Add barriers at both the front and the back of your grandstand using Nether bricks, Nether brick fences and chiseled Nether bricks.

Place three rows of quartz chairs, then add a staircase on one side, using Nether bricks and Nether brick stairs.

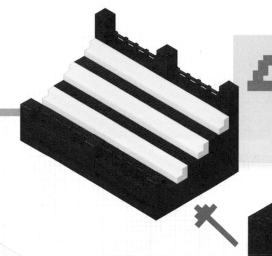

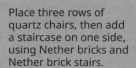

STAIRCASE

Finally, build an overhead cover using smooth quartz slabs. Add a few hanging lanterns for lighting. Repeat steps to build grandstands around your racecourse.

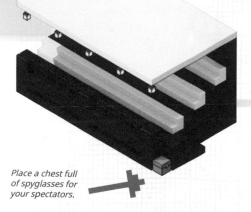

Place a chest full of spyglasses for your spectators.

FENCES

You can add fences to keep players on the racecourse.

4

Add another X formation on each side. Continue building the ladder.

5

Repeat steps 3 and 4.

6

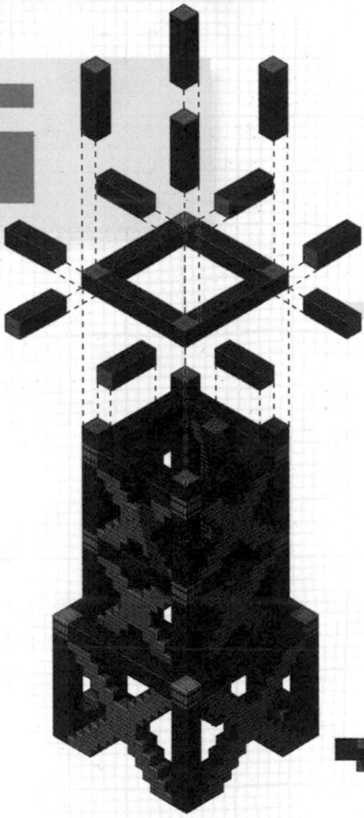

Next, create a 13x13x4 spruce log frame atop the tower as shown.

7

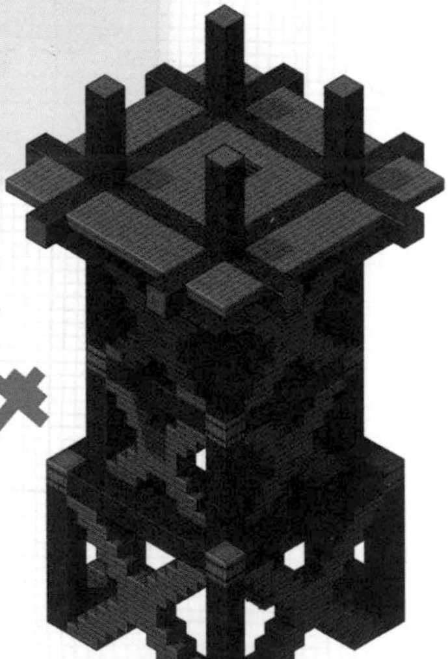

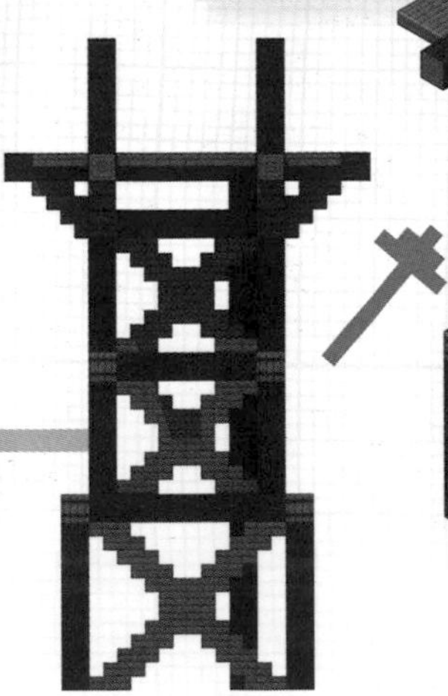

Fill in the spruce log frame with spruce slabs. Add supporting structures below the protruding beams with spruce stairs.

Use barrels, spruce slabs and outward-opening spruce trapdoors to create a handrail around the watchtower. Place another spruce trapdoor at the top of the ladder entrance.

8

9

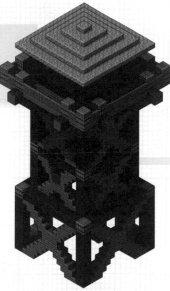

Build a roof atop the structure using cut copper stairs and slabs. Decide if you want to wax the copper while it's still shiny and orange or if you'd prefer to allow it to oxidize to blue.

BLENDING IN

A watch tower may let you spot players from afar, but it will also alert them to your whereabouts if you're not careful! Blend into the local environment with some camouflage. Add leaves to your structure to help it merge with its surroundings, or perhaps even consider different building materials if you're in a biome without lots of greenery.

SKULL COVE

Keeping your valuables safe from looting bandits requires some ingenious redstone knowledge ... or does it? Why not hide your valuables like pirates – in Skull Cove?! Though hidden in plain sight, this cave will scare off any unwanted visitors from daring to steal your treasure.

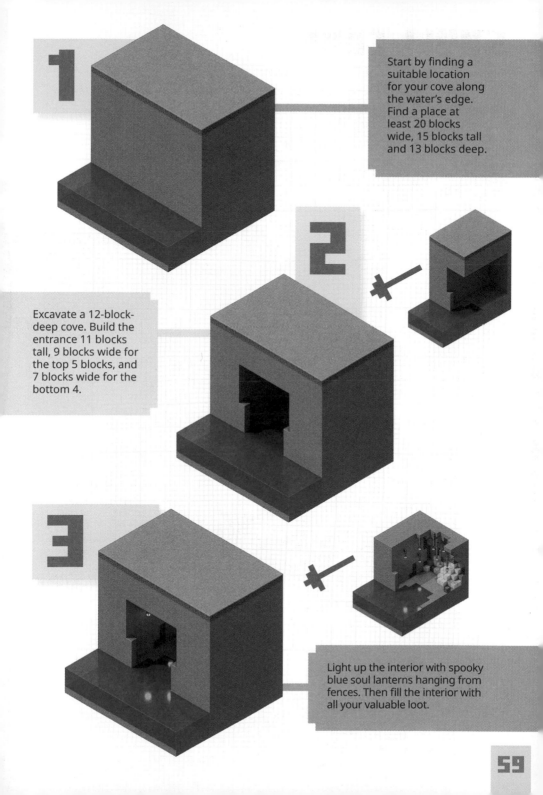

1

Start by finding a suitable location for your cove along the water's edge. Find a place at least 20 blocks wide, 15 blocks tall and 13 blocks deep.

2

Excavate a 12-block-deep cove. Build the entrance 11 blocks tall, 9 blocks wide for the top 5 blocks, and 7 blocks wide for the bottom 4.

3

Light up the interior with spooky blue soul lanterns hanging from fences. Then fill the interior with all your valuable loot.

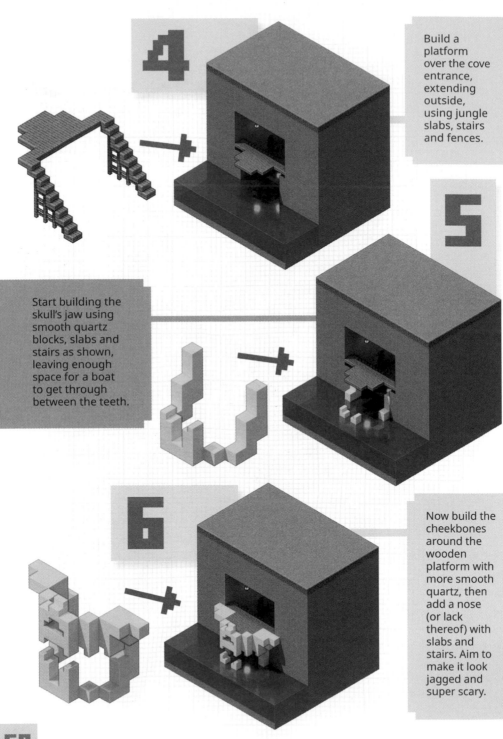

4

Build a platform over the cove entrance, extending outside, using jungle slabs, stairs and fences.

5

Start building the skull's jaw using smooth quartz blocks, slabs and stairs as shown, leaving enough space for a boat to get through between the teeth.

6

Now build the cheekbones around the wooden platform with more smooth quartz, then add a nose (or lack thereof) with slabs and stairs. Aim to make it look jagged and super scary.

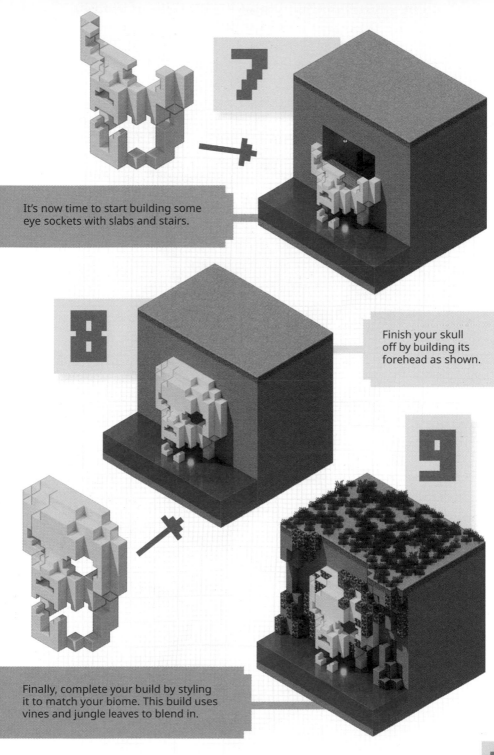

7

It's now time to start building some eye sockets with slabs and stairs.

8

Finish your skull off by building its forehead as shown.

9

Finally, complete your build by styling it to match your biome. This build uses vines and jungle leaves to blend in.

MONSTER-TRUCK BUS

Journeys to and from school have never been this much fun – or fast! The wheels on this monster-truck bus are bigger than you, meaning it can trample over any terrain in its path. Just make sure you hold on tight – it's going to be a bumpy ride. All aboard!

DIFFICULTY:
★★☆☆☆
🕐 25 mins

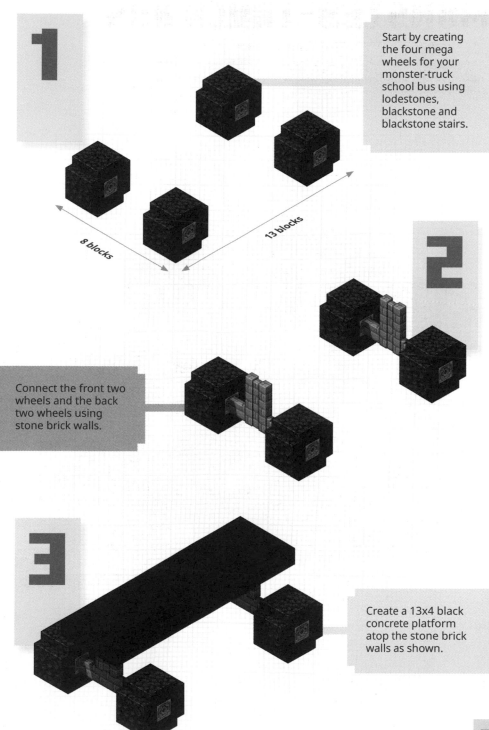

1

Start by creating the four mega wheels for your monster-truck school bus using lodestones, blackstone and blackstone stairs.

8 blocks

13 blocks

2

Connect the front two wheels and the back two wheels using stone brick walls.

3

Create a 13x4 black concrete platform atop the stone brick walls as shown.

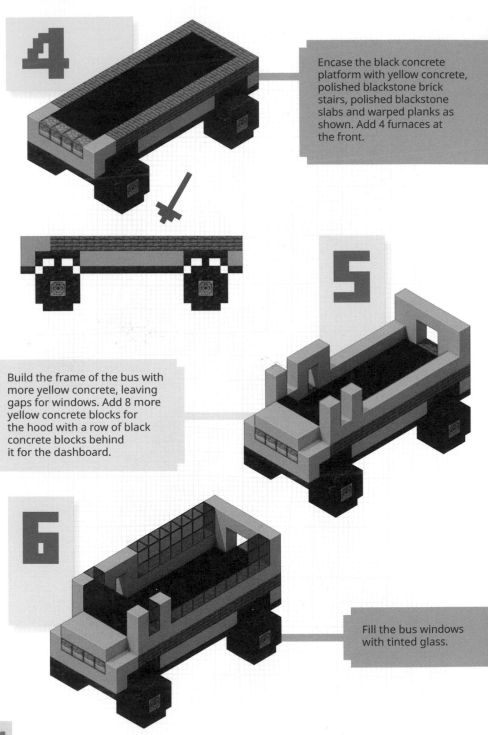

4

Encase the black concrete platform with yellow concrete, polished blackstone brick stairs, polished blackstone slabs and warped planks as shown. Add 4 furnaces at the front.

5

Build the frame of the bus with more yellow concrete, leaving gaps for windows. Add 8 more yellow concrete blocks for the hood with a row of black concrete blocks behind it for the dashboard.

6

Fill the bus windows with tinted glass.

7

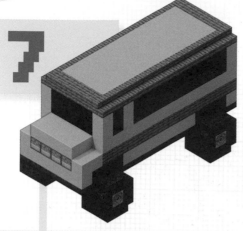

Finally, add some finishing touches to the bus. Place glow item frames as headlights, warped signs for the front grille and an iron bar and a block of redstone as an indicator light. Don't forget a ladder to climb aboard your bus!

Add a roof to the bus using more yellow concrete, warped planks and warped stairs.

8

ROTATED 180°

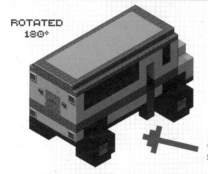

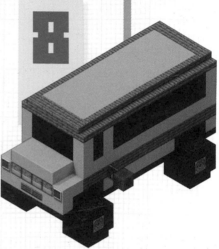

Warped doors and buttons make for the perfect back entrance. Use normal frames for a nice contrast to the glow frames at the front. Remember the ladder to get in!

INTERIOR

Monster trucks are just about as cool as school buses can get. Just imagine rocking up to the school gates in one of these! While road safety is vitally important, it's still possible to have fun while being secure.

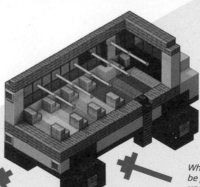

Overhead grab bars will keep you from falling over as the monster truck bounces over the biomes. End rods are perfect for those party-bus vibes – even when you're going to school.

You'll have the other school buses purring over these purpur stair seats!

Who says school buses have to be plain inside? Why not jazz it up with a pop of color?

POTION FACTORY

Potions of Healing, Potions of Strength, Potions of Swiftness ... the list goes on and on! There are plenty of different potions in Minecraft to fit every situation. Even in Creative mode, the Potion of Night Vision is super helpful. Build this factory to brew them all and find out how they work.

DIFFICULTY:

★★★★☆

🕐 35 mins

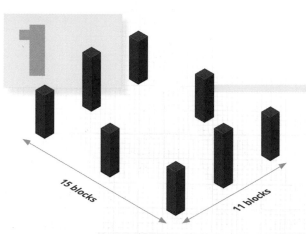

Start by building eight columns, 4 blocks tall, in a rectangle, using stripped dark oak wood, then add an extra block to the two central ones.

15 blocks

11 blocks

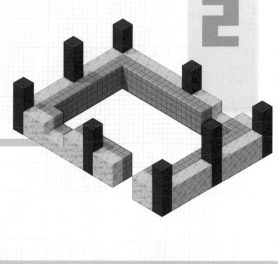

2

Fill the walls with 2-block-tall rings of calcite blocks and waxed oxidized cut copper blocks.

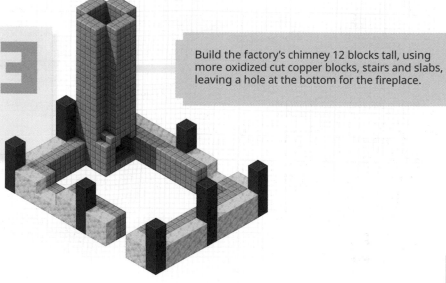

3

Build the factory's chimney 12 blocks tall, using more oxidized cut copper blocks, stairs and slabs, leaving a hole at the bottom for the fireplace.

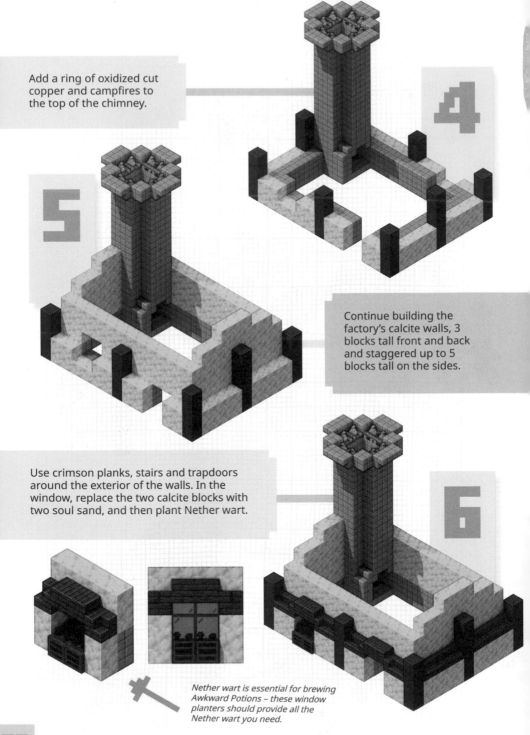

Add a ring of oxidized cut copper and campfires to the top of the chimney.

4

5

Continue building the factory's calcite walls, 3 blocks tall front and back and staggered up to 5 blocks tall on the sides.

Use crimson planks, stairs and trapdoors around the exterior of the walls. In the window, replace the two calcite blocks with two soul sand, and then plant Nether wart.

6

Nether wart is essential for brewing Awkward Potions – these window planters should provide all the Nether wart you need.

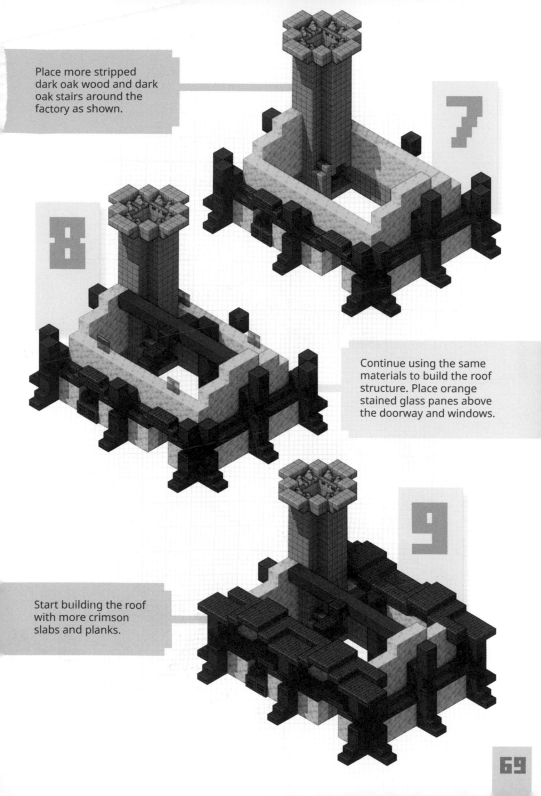

Place more stripped dark oak wood and dark oak stairs around the factory as shown.

Continue using the same materials to build the roof structure. Place orange stained glass panes above the doorway and windows.

Start building the roof with more crimson slabs and planks.

10

Finish building the roof with more of the same blocks, creating a gentle arch. Build two more, smaller, chimneys using waxed oxidized cut copper, campfires and crimson trapdoors.

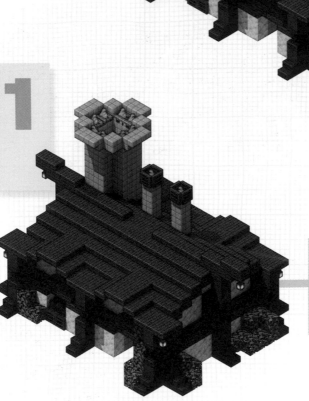

Finally, hang lanterns from each corner of the build and place flowering azalea leaves around the walls.

INTERIOR

This factory is equipped with all the essentials for brewing every potion you could ever need. So gather your ingredients and get brewing!

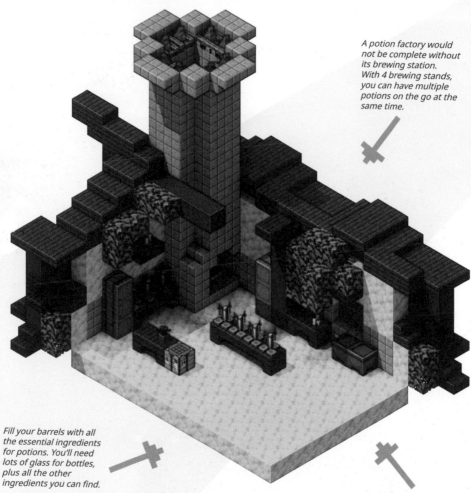

A potion factory would not be complete without its brewing station. With 4 brewing stands, you can have multiple potions on the go at the same time.

Fill your barrels with all the essential ingredients for potions. You'll need lots of glass for bottles, plus all the other ingredients you can find.

Water is an essential brewing component. Each cauldron will fill three bottles for brewing.

CAROUSEL

When it comes to fairground rides, this carousel might just be the best redstone attraction around. Take advantage of minecarts and redstone mechanics to create this amazing working carousel with rides for you and your friends. Reward the striders with some warped fungus!

DIFFICULTY:

★★★☆☆

🕒 20 mins

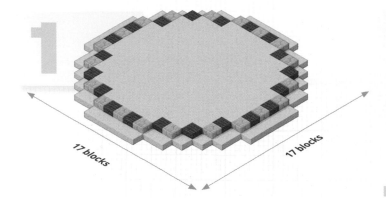

1

Start by laying the foundations for the carousel using smooth sandstone slabs, mangrove planks and prismarine bricks as shown.

17 blocks

17 blocks

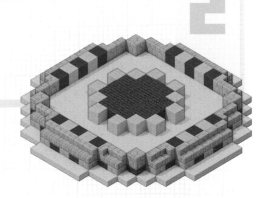

2

Next, extend the walls with prismarine blocks and stairs, red and yellow wool, and mangrove planks.

3

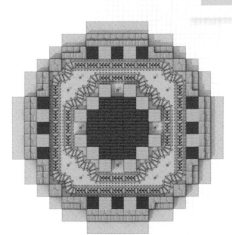

Build the redstone circuit for your carousel ride using rails, powered rails and redstone torches.

Now it's time to add the striders to your ride. Place 5 minecarts on your rails and use strider eggs to spawn 5 striders. Push your striders into the minecarts. Then give each of the striders a saddle.

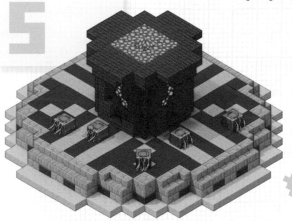

Fill the floor with red and yellow carpets and build the 5x5x5 structure in the center of the carousel using mangrove planks, stairs and fences, leaving shapes in the walls. Fill the structure with glowstone.

The minecarts continue to move even with the striders and carpets in the way!

Build a 13x13 pointed roof directly on top of the carousel using smooth sandstone and smooth sandstone stairs. Place a sandstone wall and glowstone on top.

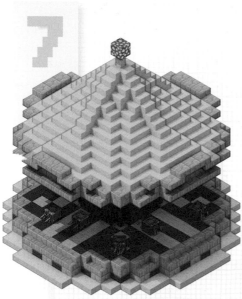

7

Add one final ring of prismarine brick blocks, stairs and slabs around the roof as shown.

Finally, illuminate the build with lanterns and End rods attached to mangrove fences.

8

LAVA PEN

Want to give your striders a place to relax? Make them feel at home with their own little lava pen, where they can go to warm up. Use the same building materials as your carousel to make the two structures match.

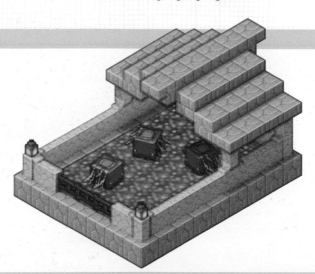

VILLAGER ISLAND HEAD

Biome explorers will be familiar with the many ancient pyramids and decrepit ruins that lay scattered throughout each dimension, but will they be familiar with the village island heads? These stone structures will have people scratching their heads to figure out who built them.

DIFFICULTY:
⭐☆☆☆☆

🕐 10 mins

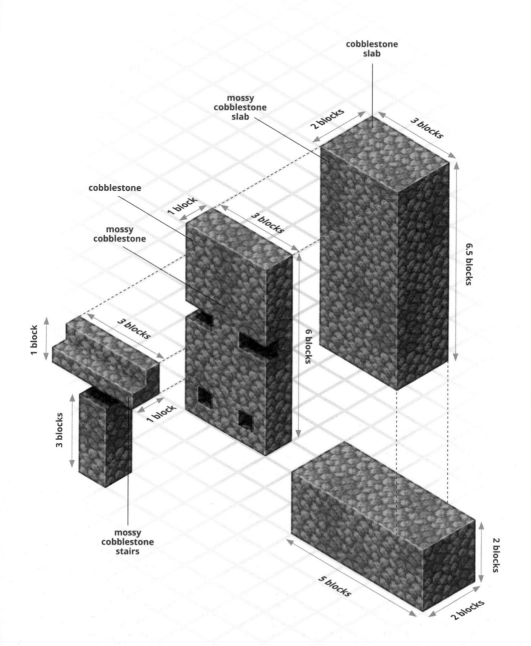

cobblestone
slab

mossy
cobblestone
slab

2 blocks

3 blocks

6.5 blocks

cobblestone

1 block

3 blocks

mossy
cobblestone

6 blocks

1 block

3 blocks

1 block

1 block

3 blocks

mossy
cobblestone
stairs

2 blocks

5 blocks

2 blocks

GIANT GRANDFATHER CLOCK

What makes this grandfather clock a bit cuckoo? The chickens that come flying out of it every morning, of course! This grandfather clock has a simple redstone circuit connecting a daylight detector and a dispenser together, so that you're woken up by birdsong every morning.

DIFFICULTY:
★★★★★
🕐 1 hour

1

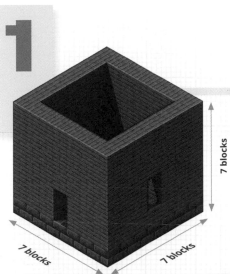

Start by creating the ground chamber for the clock tower using deepslate bricks and spruce planks. Remember to leave gaps for a doorway and a window.

7 blocks

7 blocks

7 blocks

Add more detail to the walls of the ground chamber. Create a doorway using spruce planks, stairs and a door, and a window using glass panes and spruce trapdoors for shutters.

2

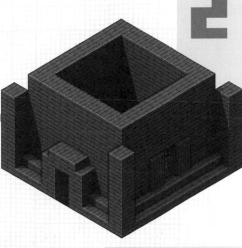

3

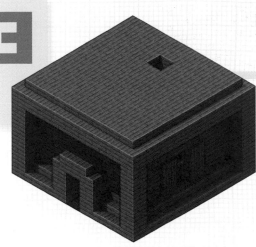

Fill in the floor above the ground chamber using more spruce planks, stairs and slabs. Leave a gap for a ladder.

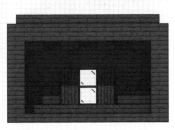

4

Next, continue building three 4-block-tall walls above the ground chamber, using more of the same blocks. Create more windows on two sides of the tower. Add a row of spruce planks along the bottom of the missing wall.

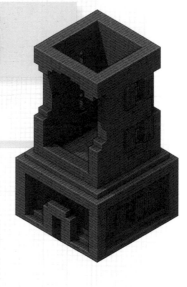

5

Continue extending the walls another 6 blocks taller as shown. Use spruce fences in the back two corners for extra detail.

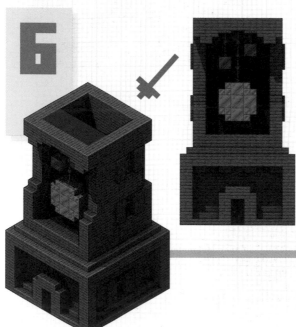

6

Now it's time to build the giant grandfather clock. Start by filling the tower with gray concrete as shown, then build the bell using waxed copper blocks, waxed cut copper stairs and lightning rods.

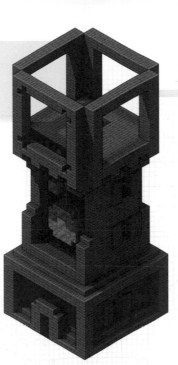

Next, continue building the clock tower another 8 blocks taller, again using spruce planks, stairs and slabs.

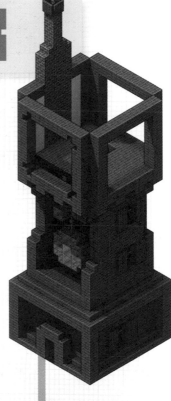

Fill in the four walls using smooth quartz, leaving gaps for windows.

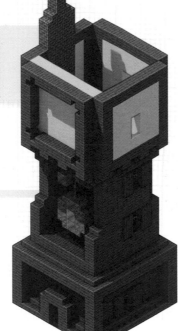

On the left-hand side of the clock tower, build a 15-block-tall chimney using brick blocks and stairs, smooth quartz, spruce trapdoors and a torch.

HOT SPRING

Ahh ... a nice, relaxing trip to the hot spring. Just what the doctor ordered! Watch your worries float away as you recline in the shallow waters, then get out and dry off beside the campfires before sheltering in the shade of the chalet for a spell. Then do it all again!

DIFFICULTY:
★★★☆☆
🕑 45 mins

1

Start by finding a flat, open area for the hot spring, ideally in a snowy biome. Then start creating the hot spring's first pond using soul sand and basalt.

23 blocks

22 blocks

The soul sand will give your hot spring's water a bubbling effect.

Add a second pond using more soul sand and basalt.

2

3

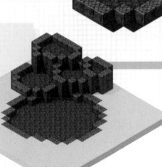

Add another three ponds using the same blocks again, each rising a block higher than the last.

4

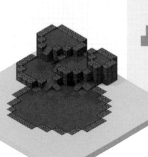

Use a water bucket to fill in the pools and remove basalt blocks to allow the water to flow down.

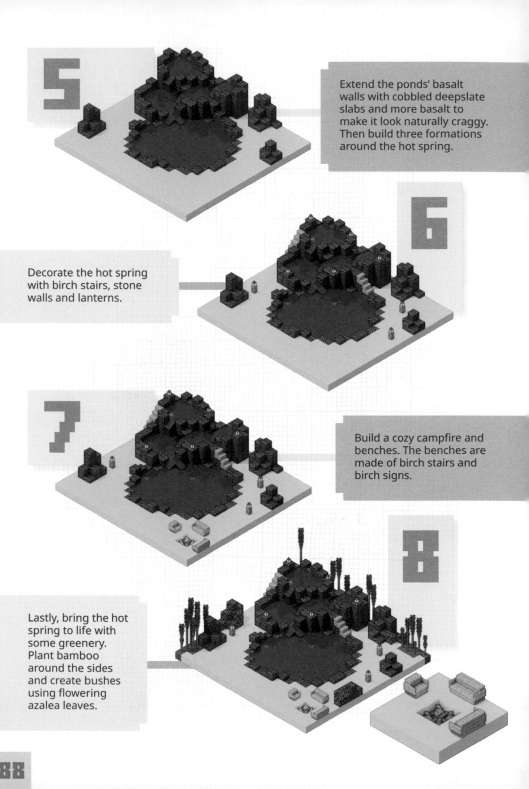

5

Extend the ponds' basalt walls with cobbled deepslate slabs and more basalt to make it look naturally craggy. Then build three formations around the hot spring.

Decorate the hot spring with birch stairs, stone walls and lanterns.

6

7

Build a cozy campfire and benches. The benches are made of birch stairs and birch signs.

8

Lastly, bring the hot spring to life with some greenery. Plant bamboo around the sides and create bushes using flowering azalea leaves.

1

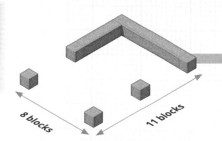

8 blocks

11 blocks

Now that the hot spring is built, create the foundation for the chalet using stripped birch logs.

Build six pillars of cobblestone blocks, 3 blocks tall at the front and 4 tall at the back. Fill the floor with birch slabs.

2

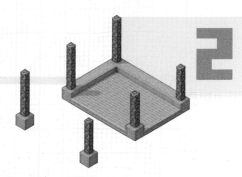

3

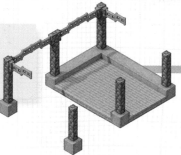

Place birch fence gates around the top of the cobblestone pillars as shown.

Finally, build a roof on top of the chalet using polished granite slabs and blocks. Then hang lanterns inside.

4

COMBINATION CHALLENGES

Congratulations, you've completed all the builds in this book. You must be quite the builder. But you're not done yet! Let's see if you're up to a new challenge: combining builds to create new ones.

Listed below is a series of combination challenges. For each of these challenges, we want you to combine the builds using the guides and build tips included in this book. How you combine the builds is completely up to you: you can resize the builds, pick new blocks or improve the design as you see fit.

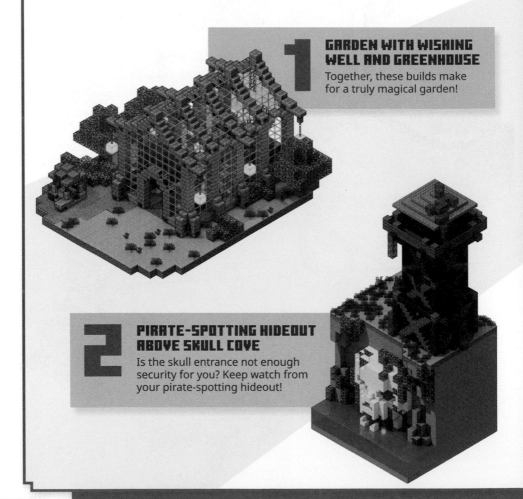

1 GARDEN WITH WISHING WELL AND GREENHOUSE
Together, these builds make for a truly magical garden!

2 PIRATE-SPOTTING HIDEOUT ABOVE SKULL COVE
Is the skull entrance not enough security for you? Keep watch from your pirate-spotting hideout!

3 MONSTER-TRUCK BUS RACETRACK

Racetracks aren't just for horses! Why not create one for your monster-truck bus?

4 STEAMBOAT TRIP TO SECRET ISLAND BASE

Travel to your secret island base in style aboard your very own steamboat!

5 PAGODA WITH HOT-SPRING BATH

You can't get more tranquil than this pagoda and hot-spring combo!

DISCOVER MORE MINECRAFT
LEVEL UP YOUR GAME WITH THE OFFICIAL GUIDES

- [ ] Guide to Combat
- [ ] Guide to Creative
- [ ] Guide to Enchantments & Potions
- [ ] Guide to Farming
- [ ] Guide to Minecraft Dungeons
- [ ] Guide to Ocean Survival

- [ ] Guide to the Nether & the End
- [ ] Guide to PVP Minigames
- [ ] Guide to Redstone
- [ ] Guide to Survival

MORE MINECRAFT:

- [ ] Amazing Bite-Size Builds
- [ ] Bite-Size Builds
- [ ] Blockopedia
- [ ] Epic Bases
- [ ] Epic Inventions
- [ ] Exploded Builds: Medieval Fortress
- [ ] Let's Build! Land of Zombies

- [ ] Let's Build! Theme Park Adventure
- [ ] Maps
- [ ] Master Builds
- [ ] Minecraft for Beginners
- [ ] Mobestiary
- [ ] The Survivors' Book of Secrets

Penguin
Random
House

DISCOVER MORE MINECRAFT
HAVE YOU READ THEM ALL?

- ☐ *The Island* by Max Brooks
- ☐ *The Crash* by Tracey Baptiste
- ☐ *The Lost Journals* by Mur Lafferty
- ☐ *The End* by Catherynne M. Valente
- ☐ *The Voyage* by Jason Fry
- ☐ *The Rise of the Arch-Illager* by Matt Forbeck
- ☐ *The Shipwreck* by C. B. Lee
- ☐ *The Mountain* by Max Brooks
- ☐ *The Dragon* by Nicky Drayden
- ☐ *Mob Squad* by Delilah S. Dawson
- ☐ *The Haven Trials* by Suyi Davies
- ☐ *Mob Squad: Never Say Nether* by Delilah S. Dawson
- ☐ *Zombies!* by Nick Eliopulos
- ☐ *Mob Squad: Don't Fear the Creeper* by Delilah S. Dawson
- ☐ *Castle Redstone* by Sarwat Chadda

Penguin
Random
House